SANGRIAS

& PITCHER DRINKS

SPECIAL THANKS to my mother-in-law, Jeannette, who gave me many of the Haasarud family recipes.

....

The publisher thanks Monin for supplying their syrups for the photography. Visit www.moninstore.com for more information.

Thanks also to thank Fabrica Home Furnishings & Upholsery LLC, 619 Vanderbilt Avenue, Brooklyn, NY 11238, 718-398-3831 for the plates on pages 13, 33, 59, and 92.

This book is printed on acid-free paper.

Published by John Wiley & Sons, Inc., Hoboken, New Jersey.
Published simultaneously in Canada.

For general information about our other products and services, please contact our Customer Care Department within the United States at (800) 762-2974, outside the United States at (317) 572-3993 or fax (317) 572-4002.

Wiley also publishes its books in a variety of electronic formats. Some content that appears in print may not be available in electronic books. For more information about Wiley products, visit our web site at www.wiley.com.

Book design by Elizabeth Van Itallie
Food styling by Mindy Fox
Prop styling by Leslie Siegel

Library of Congress Cataloging-in-Publication Data:
Haasarud, Kim.
  101 sangrias & pitcher drinks / Kim Haasarud ; Photography by Alexandra Grablewski.
    p. cm.
  Includes index.
  ISBN 978-0-470-16941-4 (cloth)
  1. Cocktails. I. Title. II. Title: One hundred and one sangrias and pitcher drinks.
  TX951.H213 2008
  641.8'74--dc22

Printed in China

10 9 8 7 6 5 4 3 2

SANGRIAS
& PITCHER DRINKS

KIM HAASARUD

PHOTOGRAPHY BY ALEXANDRA GRABLEWSKI

WILEY

JOHN WILEY & SONS, INC.

Introduction

arm Mediterranean breezes, clear azure waters, the blood red color of wine-based libations or spirits and juices mixed with fresh fruit . . . what could be better? Welcome to the wonderful world of sangrias and punches, those festive drinks for good times with great friends.

Sangria is a party-bowl concoction originally from Portugal and Spain that mixes wine, fresh fruits, and often a spirit (brandy, Grand Marnier, triple sec, vodka, rum, etc.). Red wine is the standard, but white wine and champagne can mix up a mean *sangria blanco*. The wine should be inexpensive. This is not the time for the Chateau Lafite-Rothschild; off-the-rack reds and whites will do just fine. And those "in-the-bottle" premixed sangrias? Heresy. The whole point of sangria is to find fresh fruits that blend happily and heartily with the moods of a warm outdoors. They can include any fruit that strikes one's fancy: mango, peach, grape, blackberry, raspberry, pineapple, peach, or kiwi, to name a few. This is a drink that demands fresh ingredients. But other than that, don't worry about the "right way" to make sangria. It's truly up to you. This is an opportunity to experiment and create your own signature sangria.

Like sangrias, punches can be made in large batches, from blends of five or more ingredients that include spirits, juices, and fresh fruit. Classic punches like the Singapore Sling and Curaçao Punch are included here, as well as some new ones like Provençal Punch and Watermelon Yuzu Punch. Great fun, each and every one.

My aim with the book is to give you a few communal drink ideas to get your creativity flowing and your guests geared up in happy anticipation. So go get some wine, hit the local produce market, grab a few spirits and ice, and have at it. Enjoy!

WHAT TYPES OF WINE TO USE

Red sangria is typically made with a Spanish wine like rioja. Its heartiness helps capture and hold onto the flavor of all of the various fruits. But almost any type of wine can be used. Hearty, earthy wines like Syrah, Chianti, and Sangiovese will also hold up to lots of fruits and flavors. For white sangria, I recommend a dry white like pinot grigio or sauvignon blanc.

I do not recommend using an expensive wine for sangria, because the subtleties that make a great, expensive wine so special in the first place will be lost amongst all the other flavors. There are plenty of great inexpensive wines to choose from.

HOW TO CHEAT

There are some ways to "cheat" when making a sangria. Ideally, a sangria should infuse overnight. This allows the ingredients to mingle with one another and for the fruits to impart their flavors. However, not everyone has "overnight" to wait, or even a few hours. And with fruits and berries that have tougher skin and flesh, like blueberries and apples, infusing takes quite a bit more time than with softer fruits like raspberries and peaches.

One trick is to slightly mash the fruits before mixing. This will release some of the juices into the sangria. But be careful not to mash them fully, or you'll have a mushy mess, which may not be that pretty.

Another trick is to sauté the fruits over low heat in a small amount of simple syrup (see page 6). This softens the skin and starts what I like to call the fruit "bleed." Once the fruit and berries start to soften and bleed into the simple syrup, take it off the heat, add it to the sangria mix, and stir.

GETTING MORE OUT OF YOUR FRUIT

Part of the beauty of a sangria is how enticing it looks. When cutting up the fruit, do it in ways that will make it visually appealing. Instead of cutting everything in quarters, vary the shapes and sizes. For example, cut your citrus fruits—grapefruit, lemons, limes, oranges—into wheels or half-wheels. Cut other fruits—apricots, peaches, apples, etc.—into cubes. Cut pineapples into stars, melons into balls, etc.

Simple Syrup

Simple syrup is an ingredient used often in Sangria recipes. It is a mixture of sugar to water in equal parts. Make some in advance; it can be stored in your refrigerator for weeks.

1 cup sugar
1 cup hot water

In a small bowl, glass, or empty, clean wine bottle, combine the sugar with the hot water and stir, or shake bottle, until completely dissolved. Let cool completely before using.

Fresh Sour

This recipe is used as a sweet-and-sour element in many sangria recipes. Squeeze the fruit juice immediately before using for optimum freshness.

¼ cup freshly squeezed lime juice (approximately 2 medium limes)
¼ cup freshly squeezed lemon juice (approximately 1½ lemons)
½ cup simple syrup (recipe above)

In a small bowl, glass, or empty, clean wine bottle, combine all the ingredients. Stir, or shake bottle, cover, and keep refrigerated until ready to use.

MAKES 1 CUP (OR 8 OUNCES)

FRUIT CUBES

In addition to the Tangerine Cubes used in the recipe on page 107, you can make other types of flavored ice cubes to enhance your sangrias and pitcher drinks. As the flavored ice melts, it gives the drink more flavor.

WILD BERRY CUBES

¾ cup cut-up fresh seasonal berries (e.g., blueberries, raspberries, strawberries, etc.)
1½ cups lemonade

Start with an empty 12-cube ice-cube tray and evenly distribute the fruit pieces in the cavities. Pour the lemonade into the cavities until full and freeze.

MOJITO CUBES

About 24 mint leaves
1½ cups fresh sour (see page 6)

Start with an empty 12-cube ice-cube tray and place at least 2 mint leaves in each cavity. Pour the fresh sour into the cavities until full and freeze.

1) Mom's Sangria

A classic from the kitchen of Tony Abou-Ganim's mother, Dorothy. As Tony puts it, "My mother was a wonderful cook and loved to entertain. Her culinary repertoire was full of authentic Lebanese dishes in deference to my father's native cuisine. She discovered that sangria was a perfect match for many of her meals."

....

2 bottles Spanish red wine (rioja)
12 ounces Hennessy VS cognac
12 ounces Cointreau
12 ounces freshly squeezed orange juice
8 ounces simple syrup (see page 6)
2 broken cinnamon sticks
3 to 4 lemons cut into thin wedges
3 to 4 small oranges cut into thin wedges
12 strawberries, sliced
7-Up, as needed

....

Place the wine, cognac, Cointreau, orange juice, and simple syrup in a large ceramic or glass container and stir well. Cover and refrigerate overnight. When ready to serve, pour into an ice filled pitcher to ⅔ full. Add the lemons, oranges, and strawberries, top with 7-Up, and stir gently to mix.

SERVES ABOUT 15

TIP: This tastes even better if you let it sit for 48 hours before serving! (Before adding the 7-Up.

2) SPANISH SANGRIA

....

1 bottle Spanish red wine
¼ cup cognac
¼ cup orange curaçao
¼ cup simple syrup (see page 6)
2 oranges, cut into half-wheels
2 peaches, cut into cubes
2 lemons, cut into half-wheels

....

Place all of the ingredients in a large glass or ceramic container and
stir well. Cover and refrigerate for at least 4 hours. Serve over ice in
rocks glasses. Garnish with additional fruit if desired.

SERVES ABOUT 6

3) SICILIAN SANGRIA

1 bottle Italian red wine
1 cup orange juice
½ cup orange curaçao
¼ cup simple syrup (see page 6)
2 blood oranges, cut into wedges
1 white peach, cut into wedges
1 lime, cut into half-wheels
Prosecco (Italian sparkling wine), as needed

Place all of the ingredients except the Prosecco in a large ceramic or glass container and stir well. Cover and refrigerate for at least 4 hours (best if overnight). Serve over ice in wine glasses. Garnish with additional fruit if desired. Top with a splash of Prosecco and stir.

SERVES ABOUT 7

4) SANGRIA FRANÇAIS

1 bottle Bordeaux
⅓ cup simple syrup (see page 6)
¼ cup cognac
¼ cup crème de cassis
¼ cup pomegranate juice
12 strawberries, hulled
7-Up, if desired

Place all of the ingredients except the 7-Up in a large glass or ceramic container and stir well. Cover and refrigerate for at least 4 hours. Serve over ice. Top with 7-Up, if desired, and garnish with additional strawberries.

SERVES ABOUT 7

5) Blueberry Pomegranate Sangria

1½ cups blueberries
¾ cup simple syrup (see page 6)
1 bottle red wine
1 cup pomegranate juice
¼ cup cognac
¼ cup triple sec
1 orange, cut into half-wheels (or thin wedges)

In a saucepan, combine the blueberries with the simple syrup over low heat. Cook, stirring constantly, until the blueberries start to discolor and the syrup starts to thicken, about 5 minutes. Set aside. Combine the remaining ingredients in a large ceramic or glass container. Add the blueberry mixture (liquid and berries) and stir well. Cover and refrigerate for at least 4 hours. Serve over ice.

SERVES ABOUT 7

6) Canadian Ice Wine Sangria

350 ml bottle ice wine
half a bottle (or 2 cups) dry white wine
¼ cup lemon juice
¼ cup simple syrup (see page 6)
1 green apple, cored and sliced
1 lemon, cut into wheels
1 orange, cut into half-wheels

Place all of the ingredients in a large glass or ceramic container and stir well. Cover and refrigerate for at least 4 hours (best if overnight). Serve over ice and garnish with additional fruit.

SERVES ABOUT 6

7) Raspberry Passionfruit Sangria

1 pint raspberries
½ cup simple syrup (see page 6)
1 bottle red wine
½ cup Grand Marnier
1 cup passionfruit nectar
1 orange, cut into half-wheels
1 lemon, cut into half-wheels
1 lime, cut into half-wheels

In a saucepan, combine the raspberries with the simple syrup over low heat. Stir constantly until raspberries start to soften and discolor. Set aside. Combine the remaining ingredients in a large ceramic or glass container. Add the raspberry mixture (berries and liquid) and stir well. Cover and refrigerate for at least 4 hours. Serve over ice.

SERVES ABOUT 7

8) WILDBERRY SANGRIA

¾ cup each of any three of the following berries: strawberries
   (hulled and sliced), blueberries, raspberries, blackberries,
   boysenberries (total: 2¼ cups berries)
¾ cup simple syrup (see page 6)
1 bottle red wine
½ cup triple sec
½ cup berry-flavored vodka
1 cup orange juice

In a saucepan, combine all of the berries with the simple syrup over
low heat. Stir constantly until berries just begin to soften and discolor. Set aside. Combine the remaining ingredients in a large
ceramic or glass container. Add the berry mixture (berries and liquid) and stir well. Cover and refrigerate for at least 4 hours. Serve
over ice.

SERVES ABOUT 7

9) BLACK CHERRY SANGRIA

1 bottle red wine
1 cup orange juice
1 cup black cherries, pitted and cut in half
¾ cup Monin black cherry syrup
½ cup Grand Marnier

Combine all of the ingredients in a large ceramic or glass container and stir well. Cover and refrigerate for at least 4 hours (best if overnight). Serve over ice.

SERVES ABOUT 7

1O) Fandango Sangria

Inspired by the music and dance of Spain, this sangria is a dance of various fruits and spices!

....

2 bottles of Spanish red wine
¼ cup sugar
1 red apple, cored and sliced
1 green apple, cored and sliced
1 orange, cut into wedges
1 peach, cored and sliced
1 banana, peeled and sliced
1 mango, peeled and sliced
1 cinnamon stick
12 cloves (stuck into the apple or orange pieces)
1½ liters 7-Up

....

Combine all of the ingredients except the 7-Up in a large ceramic or glass container and stir well. Cover and refrigerate for at least 4 hours (best if overnight). Just before serving, add the 7-Up. Serve over ice. Garnish with additional fruit.

SERVES ABOUT 20

11) Spicy Sangria

1 bottle red wine
1 cup orange juice (best if fresh-squeezed)
½ cup triple sec
½ cup simple syrup (see page 6)
2 limes, cut into half-wheels
1 lemon, cut into half-wheels
1 orange, cut into half-wheels
1½ teaspoons hot sauce

Combine all of the ingredients in a large ceramic or glass container and stir well. Cover and refrigerate for at least 4 hours. Serve over ice.

SERVES ABOUT 7

12) Sangria Rita

Who says you can't put tequila in a sangria? This recipe comes from one of my other books, *101 Margaritas*, but has been adapted for more servings.

1 bottle red wine
1¾ cups simple syrup (see page 6)
1⅓ cups tequila
1 orange, cut into half-wheels
1 lemon, cut into half-wheels
1 lime, cut into half-wheels

Combine all of the ingredients in a large ceramic or glass container and stir well. Cover and refrigerate for at least 4 hours. Serve over ice. If desired, shake a small amount in a cocktail shaker with ice and strain into a Margarita glass. Garnish with additional fruit.

SERVES ABOUT 7

13) SUPERBOWL SANGRIA

2 bottles of dry white wine
2 bottles of red wine
1 cup triple sec
1 cup citrus vodka
4 cups orange juice
4 oranges, cut into quarters
4 lemons, cut into wheels
4 limes, cut into wheels
2 red apples, cored and cut into wheels
2 green apples, cored and cut into wheels
2 pints strawberries, hulled and cut in half
simple syrup, to taste (see page 6)
4 liters 7-Up

Combine all of the ingredients except the 7-Up in a clean medium-sized bucket. Cover and refrigerate overnight. Just before serving, add the 7-Up. Serve over ice. If a sweeter sangria is desired, add more simple syrup to taste. Garnish with additional fruit.

SERVES ABOUT 30

14) FROZEN SANGRIA

This is a great refreshing cocktail; perfect for springtime. Feel free to use bagged frozen fruit from your local grocery store.

- **2 cups red wine**
- **2 cups frozen fruit (e.g., peaches, berries, apples, grapes, pineapple, etc.)**
- **1 cup simple syrup (see page 6)**
- **½ cup Cointreau**
- **fresh fruit pieces, for garnish**
- **½ cup 7-Up**

Combine all of the ingredients in a blender with 1 cup of ice. Blend until smooth. If a thicker consistency is desired, add more ice and blend again. Pour into cocktail glasses and garnish with fresh fruit.

SERVES ABOUT 5

15) RUM SANGRIA

12 whole cloves
2 oranges, sliced into wedges
1 apple, cored and sliced
1 bottle red wine
½ cup light rum
½ cup chopped pineapple
1 pint strawberries, hulled and sliced
2 limes, sliced into wheels
1 lemon, sliced into wheels
1 liter 7-Up

Stick the cloves in the orange wedges or apple slices. Combine the orange wedges and apple slices with all of the remaining ingredients except the 7-Up in a large ceramic or glass container and stir well. Cover and refrigerate for at least 4 hours (best if overnight). Just before serving, add the 7-Up. Serve over ice.

SERVES ABOUT 12

16) APPLE SPICE SANGRIA

1 red apple, cored and cut into chunks
1 green apple, cored and cut into chunks
1 cup apple juice
15 whole cloves
4 dashes of cinnamon
1 vanilla bean, cut lengthwise
1 bottle red wine
½ cup cognac
⅓ cup simple syrup (see page 6)
cinnamon sticks, for garnish

In a saucepan, combine the apples, apple juice, whole cloves, cinnamon, and vanilla bean over low heat. Cook, stirring constantly, until apples just begin to caramelize. Remove from heat and set aside. Let cool. Combine the wine and cognac in a large ceramic or glass container. Add the apple-spice mixture and stir well. Cover and refrigerate for at least 4 hours. Serve over ice and garnish with cinnamon sticks.

SERVES ABOUT 6

17) Candied Cranberry Orange Sangria

The perfect accompaniment to Thanksgiving dinner!

....

1½ cups whole cranberries
¾ cup simple syrup (see page 6)
1 bottle red wine
2 oranges, cut into half-wheels
½ cup cranberry juice

....

In a saucepan, combine the whole cranberries with the simple syrup over low heat. Cook, stirring constantly, until the cranberries soften and the syrup starts to thicken. Remove from the heat and set aside. Let cool. Combine the wine, oranges, and cranberry juice in a large ceramic or glass container. Add the cranberry mixture and stir well. Refrigerate for at least 4 hours. Serve over ice. Garnish with additional orange half-wheels.

SERVES ABOUT 7

18) Summer Melon Sangria

]From the Liquid Kitchen of Kathy Casey, this recipe is perfect for summer picnics and outdoor soirees.

....

    1 bottle dry white wine (such as dry riesling)
    3 teaspoons Midori melon liqueur
    2 cups peeled, seeded and cubed fresh watermelon
    2 kiwis, peeled and sliced
    1 lime, thinly sliced
    ¼ cup sugar

....

Combine all of the ingredients in a pitcher and stir, crushing some of the fruit with a spoon. Cover and refrigerate for at least 12 hours or overnight to let the flavors marry before serving. Use within 4 days of making. Serve over ice, including some of the fruit.

Serves about 6

19) WHITE PEACH SANGRIA

1 bottle Moscato d'Asti
1 cup peach nectar
¾ cup crème de peche (peach liqueur)
½ cup lemon juice
2 peaches, pitted and sliced
1 lemon, cut into half-wheels

Combine all of the ingredients in a large ceramic or glass container and stir well. Refrigerate, covered, for at least 4 hours. Serve over ice. Garnish with peach slices.

SERVES ABOUT 7

20) FROZEN PEACHY SANGRIA

Using the same ingredients as above, combine everything in a blender (except the lemons) with 2 cups of ice . Blend until smooth. Garnish with peach wedges.

SERVES ABOUT 7

21) Ambrosia Sangria

1 bottle dry white wine
¾ cup coconut rum
¼ cup vanilla syrup (such as Monin)
1 peach, pitted and sliced
1 orange, cut into half-wheels
1 cup pineapple chunks
½ cup black cherries, pitted and cut in half
7-Up, as needed (optional)

Combine all of the ingredients except the 7-Up in a large ceramic or glass container and stir well. Cover and refrigerate for at least 4 hours (best if overnight). Serve over ice. Top with 7-Up, if desired.

SERVES ABOUT 6

22) Passionate Pear Sangria

1 bottle dry white wine
½ cup Absolut Pears vodka
1 cup pear nectar
1 cup passionfruit juice
2 pears (Anjou or Bartlett), cored and sliced
2 lemons, cut into half-wheels
simple syrup, as needed (see page 6)
7-Up, as needed

Combine the white wine, pear vodka, pear nectar, passionfruit juice, and fruit in a large ceramic or glass container and stir well. Cover and refrigerate for at least 4 hours (best if overnight). If a sweeter sangria is desired, add simple syrup to taste. Serve over ice and top with 7-Up. Garnish with additional fruit.

SERVES ABOUT 7

23) SANGRIA TROPICALE

Ballatore Gran Spumante is a sparkling wine made in California
that's a bargain for the price (about $8). It is on the sweet side, and
mixes well in drinks.

1 bottle dry white wine
1 cup fresh sour (see page 6)
½ cup triple sec
1 cup pineapple chunks
2 oranges, cut into half-wheels
1 mango, sliced into 2-inch pieces
2 cups Ballatore Gran Spumante

Combine all of the ingredients except the Gran Spumante in a large
ceramic or glass container and stir well. Cover and refrigerate for at
least 4 hours. Add 2 cups Ballatore Gran Spumante. Serve over ice.
Garnish with a mango slice.

SERVES ABOUT 14

24) Pacific Blue Sangria

1 bottle dry white wine
½ cup blue curaçao
½ cup fresh lemon juice
½ cup simple syrup (see page 6)
2 oranges, cut into wheels
1 cup pineapple chunks
7-Up, as needed

Combine all of the ingredients except the 7-Up in a large ceramic or glass container and stir well. Cover and refrigerate for at least 4 hours. Serve over ice and top with 7-Up. Garnish with an orange wheel or pineapple wedge.

SERVES ABOUT 7

25) Key West Sangria

1 bottle dry white wine
½ cup SKYY Citrus vodka (or other citrus vodka)
½ cup triple sec
½ cup key lime juice (such as Nellie & Joe's)
½ cup simple syrup (see page 6)
5 limes, cut into wheels
1 cup pineapple cubes
7-Up, as needed

Combine all of the ingredients except the 7-Up in a large ceramic or glass container and stir well. Cover and refrigerate for at least 4 hours. Serve in chilled glasses and top with 7-Up. Garnish with a floating lime wheel.

SERVES ABOUT 7

26) Mango Tango Sangria

1 bottle dry white wine
½ cup light rum
¼ cup Monin mango syrup
¼ cup simple syrup (see page 6)
¼ cup lemon juice
1½ mangos, sliced into 2-inch pieces
2 lemons, cut into half-wheels
soda water or 7-Up, as needed (optional)

Combine all of the ingredients except the soda water or 7-Up in a large ceramic or glass container and stir well. Cover and refrigerate for at least 4 hours. Serve over ice and top with soda or 7-Up, if desired.

Serves about 7

27) Spicy Mango-Cilantro Sangria

1 bottle sauvignon blanc
1 cup freshly squeezed orange juice
1 cup fresh sour (see page 6)
1 cup mango nectar
½ cup triple sec
1 mango, peeled and cut into 1-inch chunks
1 cup cilantro leaves
2 jalapeños, sliced

Combine all of the ingredients in a large glass or ceramic container and stir well. Cover and refrigerate for at least 4 hours. Serve over ice. If desired, garnish with a sprig of fresh cilantro.

Serves about 8

28) TANGERINE SANGRIA

1 bottle sauvignon blanc
2 cups freshly squeezed orange juice
½ cup Cointreau
¼ cup simple syrup (see page 6)
3 tangerines, cut into thin slices
½ cup pineapple cubes
½ cup white grapes, cut in half
orange soda, as needed
orange wedges and mint sprigs, for serving (optional)

Combine all of the ingredients except the orange soda, orange wedges, and mint in a large ceramic or glass container and stir well. Cover and refrigerate for at least 4 hours. Serve in chilled cups and top with orange soda. Garnish with an orange wedge and mint sprig, if desired.

SERVES ABOUT 7

29) Watermelon Sangria

1 bottle dry white wine
¾ cup watermelon schnapps
½ cup white cranberry juice
2 cups freshly scooped watermelon balls
2 limes, cut into half-wheels

Combine all of the ingredients in a large ceramic or glass container and stir well. Cover and refrigerate for at least 4 hours. Serve over ice.

SERVES ABOUT 7

30) Pomegranate Agave Sangria

1 bottle dry white wine
1 cup pomegranate juice
1 cup fresh sour (see page 6)
½ cup pure agave reposado tequila (such as 1800 Reposado)
¼ cup Cointreau
1 orange, cut into slices
1 lemon, cut into slices
1 lime, cut into slices
1 liter 7-Up

Combine all of the ingredients except the 7-Up in a large ceramic or glass container and stir well. Cover and refrigerate for at least 4 hours. Serve over ice; fill glasses about halfway with sangria mixture, then top with 7-Up. Garnish with a lime wedge.

SERVES ABOUT 12

31) Grapefruit Grigio

1 bottle pinot grigio
½ cup gin or vodka, whichever you prefer
½ cup simple syrup (see page 6)
½ cup white grapefruit, cut into half-wheels
½ cup ruby red grapefruit, cut into quarters, then sliced
soda water, as needed

Combine all of the ingredients except the soda water in a large ceramic or glass container. Refrigerate, covered, for at least 4 hours (best if overnight). Serve over ice and top with soda water.

SERVES ABOUT 6

32) NEW ZEALAND KIWI SANGRIA

Made from New Zealand sauvignon blanc and kiwis!

1 bottle New Zealand sauvignon blanc
¼ cup Midori melon liqueur
¼ cup fresh lemon juice
¼ cup simple syrup (see page 6)
6 kiwis, peeled and sliced (use both the green and gold, for
   variation in flavor and color)
1 cup pineapple chunks
soda water or 7-Up, if desired

Combine all of the ingredients except the soda or 7-Up in a large ceramic or glass container and stir well. Cover and refrigerate for at least 4 hours. Serve over ice and top with soda or 7-Up, if desired.

SERVES ABOUT 6

33) Red, White, and Blue Sangria

1 bottle dry white wine
½ cup triple sec
¼ cup flavored vodka (citrus or berry flavored)
¼ cup fresh lemon juice
¼ cup simple syrup (see page 6)
¾ cup blueberries
¾ cup strawberries, hulled and sliced
¾ cup raspberries
½ cup pineapple chunks (optional: buy a star-shaped cookie cutter
    and cut pineapple stars out of fresh whole pineapple slices for a
    patriotic sangria)

Combine all of the ingredients in a large ceramic or glass container
and stir well. Cover and refrigerate for at least 4 hours. Serve over ice.

SERVES ABOUT 7

34) Ginger Pear Sangria

1 bottle dry white wine
½ cup white cranberry juice
¼ cup Mathilde pear liqueur
2 ripe Bartlett pears
1 piece fresh ginger (approximately 3 inches long), peeled and sliced

Combine all of the ingredients in a large ceramic or glass container
and stir well. Cover and refrigerate for at least 4 hours (best if
overnight). Serve over ice.

SERVES ABOUT 6

35) MANHATTAN SANGRIA

A cross between a Manhattan and a sangria, made with bourbon, bitters, and black cherries.

- 1 bottle red wine
- ¾ cup sweet vermouth
- ¾ cup cognac
- ½ cup simple syrup (see page 6)
- 1 teaspoon Angostura bitters
- 1 cup pitted Bing cherries

Combine all of the ingredients in a large ceramic or glass container and stir well. Cover and refrigerate for at least 4 hours. When ready to serve, strain into a cocktail shaker with ice. Shake vigorously and strain into martini glasses. Garnish with a cherry.

SERVES ABOUT 6

36) LIMONCELLO FIZZY SANGRIA

1 bottle dry white wine
2 cups lemonade
½ cup limoncello liqueur
2 lemons, cut into wheels
2 oranges, cut into wheels
1 bottle semisweet sparkling sparkling wine (e.g., Ballatore Gran
  Spumante)
20 mint sprigs, for garnish
lemon twists (or peels), for garnish

Combine the wine, lemonade, limoncello, lemons, and oranges in a large ceramic or glass container and stir well. Cover and refrigerate for at least 4 hours (best if overnight). Serve over ice; fill glasses halfway with the sangria mixture, then top with Ballatore Gran Spumante. Garnish with a mint sprig and lemon twist.

SERVES ABOUT 12

37) SONOMA GRAPE SANGRIA

1 bottle dry white wine (pinot grigio or sauvignon blanc)
1 cup white grape juice
¼ cup sugar
½ cup green grapes, cut in half
½ cup red seedless grapes, cut in half
1 orange, cut into wheels
1 lemon, cut into wheels
1 lime, cut into wheels
1 liter 7-Up

Combine all of the ingredients except the 7-Up in a large ceramic or glass container and stir well until sugar dissolves. Cover and refrigerate for at least 4 hours (best if overnight). Just before serving, add the 7-Up. Serve over ice. Garnish with speared grapes, in alternating red and green colors.

SERVES ABOUT 12

38) PACIFIC RIM SANGRIA

1 piece fresh ginger (about 2 inches long)
1 bottle (750 ml) dry sake
2 cups water
1 cup lemon juice
1 cup sugar
1 hothouse cucumber (the kind you find wrapped in plastic),
  or 4 Japanese cucumbers, cut into thin slices
strips of cucumber peel, twisted, for garnish

Preheat the oven to 350°F. Peel the ginger and loosely wrap in aluminum foil. Bake in the oven until the ginger starts to sweat, 20 to 25 minutes. Remove from the oven, and when cool enough to handle, thinly slice.

Combine the sliced ginger with the sake, water, lemon juice, sugar, and sliced cucumber in a larger ceramic or glass container and stir until the sugar is dissolved. Cover and refrigerate for at least 4 hours. Serve over ice and garnish with cucumber peels.

SERVES ABOUT 10

39) Hibiscus Sangria

1 bottle dry white wine
2 cups hibiscus tea (already steeped and cooled)
½ cup lemon juice
½ cup simple syrup (page 6)
¼ cup orange curaçao
¼ cup Hendricks gin
1 orange, sliced
1 lemon, sliced
1 liter 7-Up
thin lemon wheels, for garnish
orchids, for garnish

Combine all of the ingredients except the 7-Up and garnishes in a large ceramic or glass container and stir well. Cover and refrigerate for at least 4 hours. Serve over ice; fill glasses about half full, then top with 7-Up. Garnish with a floating lemon wheel and an orchid.

SERVES ABOUT 8

40) Spa Sangria

Champagne grapes are the tiny purple grapes—perfect for garnishes.
They are usually in season mid to late summer.

1 bottle dry white wine
2 cups fresh orange juice
½ cup triple sec
1 green apple, cored and sliced
1 cup red and green grapes, cut in half
¼ cucumber, peeled and cut into slices
1 lemon, cut into wheels
1 lime, cut into wheels
1 liter 7-Up
sage leaves, for garnish (optional)
small grape clusters, for garnish (can use regular grapes or a
    champagne grape cluster)

Combine all of the ingredients except the 7-Up and garnishes in a
large ceramic or glass container and stir well. Cover and refrigerate
for at least 4 hours. Pour into chilled glasses, filling about ¾ full.
Top with 7-Up. Garnish with 1 to 2 sage leaves, if desired, and
small grape clusters.

Serves about 8

41) KIDDIE (NON-ALCOHOLIC) SANGRIA

3 cups white cranberry juice (can also use white grape juice)
3 cups orange juice
½ cup Monin red sangria syrup
½ cup lemon juice
1 lemon, cut into wheels
1 orange, cut into wheels
1 apple, cored and sliced
½ cup pineapple cubes
7-Up, as needed

Combine all of the ingredients in a large pitcher and stir well. Cover and refrigerate for at least 2 hours. Pour into chilled glasses and top with 7-Up. Add additional fruit for garnish, if desired.

SERVES ABOUT 7

42) Sangria Cocktail

1 bottle red wine
½ cup citrus vodka
½ cup Cointreau
¾ cup pineapple juice
2 oranges, cut into quarters
1 lemon, cut into half-wheels
1 lime, cut into half-wheels
7-Up, as needed
skewered fruit, for garnish (e.g., grapes or pineapple chunks)

Combine all of the ingredients except the 7-Up and skewered fruit in a large ceramic or glass container and stir well. Cover and refrigerate for at least 4 hours. When ready to serve, strain the sangria into a cocktail shaker with ice. Shake vigorously and strain into chilled cocktail or wine glasses. Top with 7-Up and garnish with skewered fruit.

Serves about 7

43) "Made to Order" Classic Sangria (or Sangria Cup)

Sometimes we just don't have time to wait overnight or several hours for a sangria to infuse properly. This recipe will give you a nice sangria without the wait. It may not be as fruity, but it is tasty.

....

3 ounces red wine
¾ ounce cognac
1½ ounces pineapple juice
2 orange slices
2 lime slices
2 lemon slices
soda water or 7-Up, as needed

....

Combine all of the ingredients except the soda water or 7-Up in a cocktail shaker with ice. Shake vigorously and pour into a large glass. Top with soda water or 7-Up and garnish with additional fruit, if desired.

Serves 1

SANGAREE

The sangaree predates the sangria and is thought to be its predecessor. A sangaree is usually whiskey- or brandy-based and includes some kind of wine, sugar, and spice (usually nutmeg or cinnamon). It is also a fairly strong drink, not fruity and sweet like the sangria.

44) WHISKEY SANGAREE

This is a slight variation from the classic that is very smooth.

....

    1½ ounces blended whiskey (Crown Royal is a good choice)
    1 ounce tawny port
    1 ounce simple syrup (see page 6)
    splash of fresh lemon juice
    soda water, as needed
    lemon peel, for garnish
    ground cinnamon, for garnish
    ground nutmeg, for garnish

....

Combine the whiskey, port, simple syrup, and lemon juice in a cocktail shaker with ice. Shake moderately and strain into chilled cocktail glass. Top with a splash of soda water, garnish with a large piece of lemon peel, and dust with cinnamon and nutmeg.

SERVES 1

45) SHERRY SANGAREE

2 ounces amontillado sherry
½ ounce honey liqueur
orange peel, for garnish
ground nutmeg, for garnish

Combine the sherry and honey liqueur in a cocktail shaker with ice. Shake vigorously and strain into a cocktail or cordial glass. Garnish with orange peel and dust with nutmeg.

SERVES 1

46) Peach Sangaree

1½ ounces peach brandy
1 ounce simple syrup (see page 6)
1 ounce tawny port
2 peach slices
ground cinnamon or nutmeg, for garnish

Combine the peach brandy, simple syrup, and port in a cocktail shaker with ice. Shake moderately and strain into a cocktail glass. Garnish with 2 peach slices and dust with nutmeg or cinnamon.

Serves 1

47) Apricot Sangaree

Use the same recipe as above, substituting apricot brandy for the peach brandy.

Cups

Cups are beverages made from a combination of seasonal fruits, juice, and a spirit. The fruit should impart its essence into the drink and not be completely infused. The fruit flavors should be fairly subtle. Almost any fruit can be used, but cups almost always include cucumber and mint.

48) Pimm's Cup

Pimm's No. 1 is a gin-based beverage popular in Great Britain. This is a great, refreshing summer cocktail. Traditionally, it is served with just a floating cucumber, but many variations include seasonal fruit. I prefer to shake everything together to impart more of the fruit, cucumber, and mint flavor into the drink. Feel free to add an additional garnish, if desired.

....

4 ounces lemonade
2 ounces Pimm's No. 1
1 to 3 cucumber slices
optional fruit: 2 orange wheels, 2 lemon wheels, 2 apple slices
ginger ale, as needed
mint sprig, for garnish

....

Combine the lemonade, Pimm's, cucumber slices, and fruit, if desired, in a cocktail shaker with ice. Shake moderately and pour into a large glass. Top with a splash of ginger ale and garnish with a mint sprig. This recipe can be multiplied by six and made in a pitcher.

SERVES 1

49) ITALIAN CUP

3 ounces fresh sour (see page 6)
1 ounce vodka
½ ounce Campari
½ ounce simple syrup (see page 6)
any 3 of the following fruit: blood oranges, naval oranges,
   strawberries, lemon wheels, lime wheels, strawberries
3 cucumber half-wheels
mint sprig
Prosecco (Italian sparkling wine), as needed

Combine all of the ingredients except the Prosecco in a cocktail
shaker with ice. Shake moderately and pour contents into a large
glass. Top with Prosecco.

SERVES 1

50) TEQUILA CUP

3 ounces fresh sour (see page 6)
1½ ounces 1800 Silver tequila
½ ounce orange curaçao
3 cucumber half-wheels
1 strawberry, hulled
3 mint leaves
7-Up, as needed
optional fruit: peach, apple, pear, tangerine, berries, etc.

Combine all of the ingredients in a cocktail shaker with ice. Shake
moderately and pour contents into a large glass. Top with a splash of
7-Up. Serve with a straw.

SERVES 1

51) CHOPIN PLAYER'S CUP

I've served this cocktail at about half a dozen events across the U.S., and it has always been a huge hit. The cocktail can change as the seasons change, featuring various fruits and berries as appropriate.

1½ ounces Chopin vodka
1 ounce Grand Marnier
¾ ounce lime juice
any of the following fruit: pear slices, red and green apple slices,
    raspberries, blueberries, blackberries, strawberries
cucumber slices
mint sprigs
ginger ale, as needed
Angostura bitters

Combine all of the ingredients except the ginger ale and bitters in a cocktail shaker with ice. Shake vigorously and pour contents into a highball glass. Top with ginger ale and a dash of bitters. Garnish with an additional mint sprig, if desired. This cocktail can also be prebatched in large portions.

SERVES 1

52) Barefoot Beach Cup

This is a great easy-to-make cocktail that's perfect for the beach.
You can prep everything in advance and add the bubbly right before
serving. Feel free to add or substitute any seasonal fruit you find at
your local grocery store.

....

3 ounces fresh sour (see page 6)
1 strawberry, hulled and sliced
4 grapes, cut in half
3 orange slices
4 to 5 mint leaves
⅓ cup Barefoot Bubbly Brut Cuvee (a light sparkling wine found in
   most liquor stores and markets)

....

Combine all of the ingredients except the Barefoot Bubbly in a
cocktail shaker with ice. Shake vigorously and pour into large pint
glass or beach cup. Fill with additional ice and top off with Barefoot
Bubbly. (If making a batch in advance, combine all of the fruit with
the fresh sour, cover, and keep chilled until ready to serve.)

SERVES 1

53) SANGRITA

A sangrita is a tomato-based cocktail served with tequila. It's the Mexican version of the Bloody Mary and can be made with a variety of savory ingredients. It is often served without alcohol alongside a shot of tequila. Some recipes call for grenadine or sugar—use these if you prefer a sangrita that's on the sweeter side. Personally, I like a more savory one.

¼ cup fresh lime juice
2 teaspoons chopped onion
2 teaspoons hot sauce
2 teaspoons Worcestershire sauce
salt and freshly ground black pepper to taste
2 cups tomato juice
1 cup orange juice
shot of pure agave tequila (a silver tequila is preferable, because its agave bite complements the spicy sangrita)
lime wedges, for serving

Combine the lime juice, onion, hot sauce, Worcestershire, and salt and pepper in a blender. Blend until smooth. In a pitcher, combine the blended mixture with the orange juice and tomato juice. Chill. When ready to serve, stir well, pour into small glasses, and pour tequila into separate shot glasses. Drink the tequila, suck on a lime wedge, and chase it with the sangrita.

SERVES ABOUT 7

54) RED PEPPER SANGRITA

2½ ounces Pepper Mix (see below)
1½ ounces pure agave silver tequila
whole red chili pepper, for garnish

Combine the Pepper Mix and tequila in a cocktail shaker with ice. Stir well (about ten seconds), strain into a chilled martini glass, and garnish with the red chili pepper.

SERVES 1

PEPPER MIX

¾ cups tomato juice
¼ cup fresh sour (see page 6)
¼ cup roasted red pepper puree (Perfect Puree makes a good one, or roast your own red peppers and blend in a blender until smooth)
freshly ground black pepper, to taste
Habanero Tabasco, to taste

Combine all of the ingredients in a pitcher and stir until mixed.

SERVES 4

55) MANGO SANGRITA

1½ ounces silver tequila
2 ounces tomato juice
1 ounce mango puree
1 ounce fresh sour (see page 6)
1 teaspoon Tabasco

Combine all of the ingredients in a cocktail shaker with ice and stir contents. Strain into shot glass or martini glass.

SERVES 1

PUNCHES

Looking for a punch for a special occasion? You are sure to find it among the following recipes. They range from classics like the Singapore Sling, to bridal punches such as the Pink Petal Punch, to a wintertime Milk Punch.

56) SINGAPORE SLING

One of the all-time classic punches, created at the Raffles Hotel in the early 1900s.

.....

1½ ounces gin (a higher proof gin like Tanqueray is a great choice)
½ ounce Cherry Heering brandy
¼ ounce Benedictine (or B&B)
¼ ounce triple sec
¼ ounce fresh lime juice
3 ounces pineapple juice (name-brand or freshly juiced)
soda water, as needed
Angostura bitters
skewered orange wedge and maraschino cherry, for garnish

.....

Combine the gin, brandy, Benedictine, triple sec, lime juice, and pineapple juice in a cocktail shaker with ice. Shake vigorously and strain into a highball glass filled with ice. Top with splash of soda, add a dash of bitters, and garnish with a skewered orange chunk and cherry (also called a flag).

SERVES 1

57) Picon Punch

Adapted from a recipe in Ted Haigh's book, *Vintage Spirits and Forgotten Cocktails* (Quarry Books, 2004), this is a very classy, tasty punch that originated in Bakersfield, California. According to Haigh, the original Amer Picon can no longer be found, but adding a dash of orange bitters brings one very close to the original.

2½ ounces Torani Amer (if this special spirit cannot be found at your local liquor store, go to www.bevmo.com or www.wineglobe.com)
1 teaspoon grenadine
soda water, as needed
1 ounce brandy
orange bitters
maraschino cherry, for garnish (optional)

Fill a highball glass with ice. Add the Torani Amer and grenadine. Fill with soda water. Top with float of brandy, add a dash of bitters, and garnish with a cherry, if desired.

Serves 1

58) Mai Tai

The Mai Tai was created by Victor J. "Trader Vic" Bergeron who owned and operated Trader Vics in southern California. On the Trader Vic's website, they list a recipe using their own Mai Tai mix, but I prefer to build this cocktail from scratch, like the original.

2 ounces Jamaican rum (dark)
½ ounce orgeat syrup (an almond syrup found at most liquor stores)
¾ ounce orange curaçao
juice of 1 lime
splash (¼ ounce) of simple syrup (see page 6)
lime wedge, for garnish
mint sprig, for garnish

Combine all of the ingredients except the garnishes in a cocktail shaker with ice. Shake vigorously and strain into a cocktail glass filled with ice. Garnish with a lime wedge and mint sprig.

Serves 1

59) Curaçao Punch

Adapted from a recipe in Ted Haigh's book, *Vintage Spirits and Forgotten Cocktails* (Quarry Books, 2004).

....

    1 teaspoon sugar
    1 ounce soda water
    2 to 3 dashes fresh lemon juice
    2 ounces orange curaçao
    1 ounce brandy
    1 ounce Bacardi 8 rum
    1 orange wheel, for garnish

....

Dissolve the sugar in the soda water and lemon juice in a cocktail glass. Fill with crushed ice. Add the orange curaçao, brandy, and rum and stir well. Garnish with orange wheel.

SERVES 1

60) Milk Punch

This classic can also be made with brandy instead of bourbon.

....

    2 ounces bourbon
    1 teaspoon dark rum
    ½ ounce simple syrup (see page 6)
    2 dashes vanilla extract
    2 ounces half-and-half
    1 ounce whole milk
    ground nutmeg, for garnish

....

Combine all of the ingredients except the nutmeg in a cocktail shaker with ice. Shake vigorously and strain into a chilled cocktail glass. Dust with nutmeg.

SERVES 1

61) MACADAMIA NUT BRULEE

This is a variation on the classic Milk Punch (see previous recipe), made with several different spirits and topped with crushed macadamia nuts.

....

2½ ounces light cream (or half-and-half)
¾ ounce Baileys Irish Cream
¾ ounce Navan vanilla liqueur
¾ ounce Hennessy cognac
½ ounce simple syrup (see page 6)
1 tablespoon crushed macadamia nuts

....

Combine all of the ingredients except the macadamia nuts in a cocktail shaker with ice. Shake vigorously and loosely strain into a cocktail glass. There should be a nice layer of foam on the top of the drink. Sprinkle the macadamia nuts on top of the foam and serve.

SERVES 1

62) APPLEBOWL PUNCH

If desired, substitute a sweet sparkling wine for the 2 cups of ginger ale.

....

    2 quarts apple cider
    2 cups cranberry juice
    2 teaspoons lemon juice
    3 red apples and 3 green apples, cored and sliced
    4 cups ginger ale

....

Combine the juices and fruit in a punch bowl. Cover and chill for at least 2 hours. Before serving, add the ginger ale (or sweet sparkling wine). Add either ice cubes or an "ice ring," made by freezing water in a ring mold.

SERVES ABOUT 15

63) CRANTUCKET PUNCH

This punch is alcohol-free, but you can spike it with berry-flavored vodka or rum, if you prefer.

....

    2 quarts cranberry juice
    1 quart apple juice
    1 teaspoon almond extract
    4 oranges, cut into slices
    6 cups 7-Up or ginger ale

....

To make a cranberry ice ring, put 1 to 2 bags of whole cranberries in a ring mold. Fill with water and freeze. Combine the cranberry and apple juices, almond extract, and orange slices in a punch bowl and stir well. Cover and chill for at least 2 hours. Just before serving, add the cranberry ice ring and the 7-Up or ginger ale.

SERVES ABOUT 20

64) SUMMERTIME CITRUS PUNCH

22 quarts lemonade
1 quart pineapple juice
4 cups citrus vodka (optional)
4 lemons, cut into slices
5 limes, cut into slices
8 to 10 pineapple rings
6 cups 7-Up or ginger ale

Combine all of the ingredients except the 7-Up or ginger ale in a punch bowl and stir well. Cover and chill for at least 2 hours. Just before serving, add the 7-Up or ginger ale and ice.

SERVES ABOUT 25

65) Banana Berry Punch

6 bananas, ripe
3 pints fresh raspberries
one 12-ounce can frozen orange juice concentrate
one 6-ounce can frozen lemon juice concentrate
2 cups pineapple juice
2 cups water
2 quarts 7-Up
berry-flavored vodka or rum (optional)

In a blender, combine the bananas, 2 pints of the raspberries, the juice concentrates and pineapple juice, and water and blend until smooth. Transfer to a bowl, cover, and freeze overnight. Remove from freezer 2 hours before serving. Mix with the 7-Up in a punch bowl just before serving. Float the remaining fresh raspberries in the punch. If desired, add an ounce of berry-flavored rum or vodka to each serving.

Serves about 16

66) Tutti Frutti Punch

one 6-ounce can frozen orange juice concentrate, thawed
¼ cup fresh lemon juice
½ cup pineapple juice
1 ounce grenadine
2 pints lemon sorbet
3 cups ginger ale
1 cup citrus or orange vodka (optional, for a spiked version)
2 pints fresh strawberries, cut in half
3 lemons, cut in half-wheels
mint sprigs, for garnish

Combine the orange juice concentrate, lemon juice, pineapple juice, and grenadine in a large container and stir well. Cover and refrigerate for at least 2 hours. Pour into a punch bowl. Using a melon baller or small ice cream scoop, ball the lemon sorbet into the mixture. Add the ginger ale and vodka (if desired), and garnish with the strawberries, lemons, and mint.

SERVES ABOUT 16

67) WATERMELON YUZU PUNCH

Yuzu is an Asian fruit that is commonly used in Japanese cuisine as a seasoning. It is extremely tart and tastes like a lemon crossed with a grapefruit and mandarin orange.

....

1 medium-sized ripe watermelon
2 quarts lemonade
¼ cup yuzu juice
1 liter 7-Up
4 cups Bacardi Gran Melon or a citrus vodka (optional)

....

Cut off ⅓ of the watermelon. De-seed and use a melon baller to scoop out balls. Place the melon balls in a bowl and freeze. De-seed the remainder of the watermelon and scoop the flesh into a blender. Blend and transfer the juice to a large container. Add the lemonade and yuzu juice and stir well. Cover and refrigerate until cold. Before serving, add the frozen melon balls and 7-Up. Add Bacardi Gran Melon or citrus vodka, if desired.

SERVES ABOUT 14

68) RAZZBERRY SORBET PUNCH

2 cups orange juice
2 cups pineapple juice
½ cup lemon juice
2 liters ginger ale
½ gallon raspberry sorbet, soft
½ cup rum or vodka (optional, for a spiked version)
2 pints fresh raspberries, for garnish
mint sprigs, for garnish

Combine the rum or vodka, orange juice, pineapple juice, and lemon juice in a large container and stir well. Cover and refrigerate for at least 2 hours. Just before serving, stir in the ginger ale. Spoon the sorbet into small scoops and add to the mixture. The sorbet will float and slowly start to melt. Garnish with the fresh raspberries and mint sprigs.

SERVES ABOUT 30

69) PROVENÇAL PUNCH

8 cups white cranberry juice
1 cup Marie Brizard Parfait Amour (a lavender-colored spirit)
2 cups fresh lemon juice
2 cups simple syrup (see page 6)
2 cups red and white grapes, cut in half
3 lemons, cut into half-wheels
3 limes, cut into half-wheels
lavender sprigs, for garnish

Combine all of the ingredients except the lavender sprigs in a large ceramic or glass container and stir well. Cover and refrigerate for at least 4 hours. Pour into glasses and garnish each serving with a lavender sprig.

SERVES ABOUT 14

70) SAKE PUNCH

This recipe is from *Dishing with Kathy Casey: Food, Fun and Cocktails from Seattle's Culinary Diva* (Seattle: Sasquatch Books, 2002).

1 (750 ml) bottle sake
6 teaspoons honey
1 lemon, thinly sliced
1 large tangerine or orange, thinly sliced
1 large black or red plum, pitted and thinly sliced into wedges
   (substitute 2 apricots or 1 sliced peach or nectarine if plums
   are not available)
2-inch piece fresh ginger, peeled and thinly sliced
1 stalk fresh lemongrass, split in half lengthwise, then cut into
   3- to 4-inch pieces

In a pitcher, combine all of the ingredients and stir with a spoon, crushing some of the fruit. Cover and refrigerate overnight or for at least 12 hours, to let the flavors marry. Use within 4 days of making. Serve over ice, including some of the fruit in each serving.

SERVES ABOUT 6

KATHY'S TIP: An inexpensive dry sake definitely works in this recipe. For truly sublime refreshment, however, try it at least once with a premium *junmai* sake. I use Momokawa Silver sake, which is fragrant with notes of pears, citrus, and even a hint of watermelon rind. *Kampai!*

71) PINK PETAL PUNCH

This can also be called Bridal Bowl or Baby Bowl—great for showers. Be sure to use organic rose petals, free of pesticides or other chemicals.

....

4 cups pink lemonade (made from concentrate is fine)
1 cup Monin rose syrup
1 cup lemon juice
½ cup rose petals
2 to 3 lemons, cut into wheels
7-Up, as needed
citrus vodka (optional)

....

Combine the pink lemonade, rose syrup, and lemon juice in a large pitcher and stir well. Cover and refrigerate until ready to serve. Just before serving, stir in the lemon wheels and rose petals. Serve over ice; fill glasses about half full, then top with 7-Up. If desired, add a shot of citrus vodka. Garnish each serving with additional rose petals and a lemon wheel.

SERVES ABOUT 7

72) FRESH LEMONADE

4 cups fresh lemon juice
4 cups simple syrup (see page 06)
flavored vodka (optional, as desired)
2 lemons, cut into wheels
mint sprigs, for garnish (optional)

Combine the lemon juice and simple syrup in a large container and stir well. Chill until ready to serve. (For a slushy version, freeze for several hours, stirring every hour.) Just before serving, pour vodka into individual glasses, if desired, and top with the lemonade mixture. Garnish with lemon wheels and mint sprigs, if desired.

SERVES ABOUT 8

73) WILDFIRE LEMONADE

Use the same recipe as above, but top off each serving with an ounce of pomegranate juice. The juice should cascade down the sides of the glass. Garnish with lemon wheels.

74) Strawberry Basil Lemonade

2 quarts pink lemonade
2 pints strawberries, hulled and cut into slices
12 whole basil leaves
3 cups citrus vodka (optional)

Combine the lemonade, strawberries, and basil leaves in a large container and stir well. Add the vodka, if desired. Cover and refrigerate for at least 2 hours. Serve over ice, garnishing each glass with an additional strawberry and fresh basil leaf.

SERVES ABOUT 10

75) Lemon Berry Pitcher Punch

1 quart lemonade
1 cup cran-raspberry juice
1 pint blueberries
1 pint raspberries
2 cups citrus- or berry-flavored vodka (optional)
1½ cups 7-Up
24 or more fruit cubes, if desired (see page 7)

Combine the lemonade, cran-raspberry juice, blueberries, and raspberries in a large pitcher and stir well. Stir in the vodka, if desired. Cover and refrigerate for at least 2 hours. Just before serving, add the 7-Up and fruit cubes. Feel free to add more vodka if you desire a stronger drink.

SERVES ABOUT 8

76) MELON BALL LEMONADE

2 quarts lemonade
1 honeydew or cantaloupe, de-seeded and balled
4 to 5 lemons, cut into half-wheels
3 cups Bacardi Gran Melon (optional)

Combine all of the ingredients in a large container and stir well.
Cover and refrigerate for at least 2 hours. Serve over ice.

SERVES ABOUT 10

77) PEACH BASIL SWEET TEA

1 gallon water
12 orange pekoe tea bags
2 cups basil leaves
1 cup simple syrup, or more to taste (see page 6)
3 quarts peach nectar
flavored vodka or peach schnapps (optional)
fresh peach slices, for garnish

In a large pot, bring the water to a boil. Add the tea bags and basil leaves and let steep for about 15 minutes. Add the simple syrup and let cool. Add the peach nectar, cover, and chill for at least 2 hours. Serve over ice and garnish with fresh peach slices and basil leaves. Add an ounce or two of flavored vodka or peach schnapps to each serving, if desired. (A little lighter on the peach schnapps, for it will be much stronger in flavor.)

SERVES ABOUT 30

78) MANGO GUAVA TEA

Use the same recipe as above, substituting guava and mango nectar for peach nectar and omitting the basil. Garnish with a mint sprig, lemon wheel, and mango slice, if desired. If using alcohol, use a flavored vodka. (Peach schnapps may be overpowering.)

79) CREAMY DREAMY ORANGEADE

6 ounces frozen orange juice concentrate
¾ cup half-and-half (or light cream)
½ cup of water
½ cup simple syrup (see page 6)
2 ounces vanilla-flavored vodka (or Navan vanilla liqueur, for a richer flavor)

Combine all of the ingredients in a blender with 3 to 4 ice cubes. Blend until smooth. The mixture should not be overly thick. Serve in small cups.

SERVES 2

80) Raspberry Arnold Palmer

½ cup lemonade
½ cup iced tea
5 to 7 fresh raspberries, plus extra for garnish
1 to 1½ ounces berry-flavored vodka (optional)
mint sprig, for garnish

Combine the lemonade and iced tea in a cocktail shaker with ice. Add the raspberries and shake well. Pour into a glass. If desired, add the berry-flavored vodka. Garnish with a mint sprig and additional whole raspberries.

Serves 1

81) Agave Limeade

6 ounces frozen limeade concentrate
1 cup water
2 ounces pure agave reposado tequila
1 ounce triple sec
lime half-wheels, for garnish (optional)

Combine all of the ingredients except the lime half-wheel in a blender with 4 to 5 ice cubes. Blend until smooth. The mixture should not be too thick. Pour into small cups and garnish each with a lime half-wheel.

SERVES ABOUT 2

82) Mojito Limeade

Use the same recipe as above, blending in ¾ cup mint leaves and substituting 3 ounces light rum for the tequila and triple sec.

SERVES ABOUT 2

83) JERRY'S HOUSE COCKTAIL

This cocktail was created by a good friend of mine, Jerry Hirschman, in Palm Springs, California. He has a tangerine tree in his backyard and uses its fruit to make fresh tangerine cubes. This is an easy-to-make and refreshing summertime drink, the perfect way to cool off guests in the hot sun. The longer the drink sits out, the better it gets!

12 tangerines (or regular oranges), for tangerine cubes (see below)
7-Up, as needed
orange- or citrus-flavored vodka, as needed
tangerine slices and mint sprigs, for garnish (optional)

To make tangerine cubes, squeeze the juice from tangerines (or oranges) into an empty ice tray and let freeze. Once the cubes are frozen, drop them into tall glasses. Fill a third to half of each glass with orange or citrus vodka, depending on how strong you like your drink. Top with 7-Up and serve. If desired, garnish with a couple of tangerine slices and a mint sprig.

SERVES 3 TO 4

84) CLEMENTINE BLOSSOM COOLER

6 cups orange juice
2 cups Hangar One Mandarin Blossom vodka
1 cup fresh lemon juice
7-Up
12 clementine slices
12 long mint sprigs

Combine the orange juice, vodka, and lemon juice in a large container and stir well. Cover and refrigerate until chilled. Pour into chilled highball glasses until about ¾ full. Top with 7-Up. Garnish with clementine slices and mint sprigs.

SERVES ABOUT 12

85) SPICED TEA

¼ cup whole cloves
2½ teaspoons ground cinnamon
3 teaspoons ground cardamom
2 teaspoons ground nutmeg
2 teaspoons grated fresh ginger
½ teaspoon ground allspice (or about 1 teaspoon whole allspice)
¼ pound loose tea (Earl Grey or orange pekoe)
¼ cup grated orange zest
1 gallon water
spiced rum, as needed

Combine the cloves, cinnamon, cardamom, nutmeg, ginger, and all-spice in a spice blender or food processor and process until ground. Combine the tea, orange zest, and ground spices in a large tea strainer/steeper. In a large pot, bring the water to a boil, then remove from heat. Add the tea strainer/steeper and steep for approximately 10 minutes. Discard the tea and serve hot or over ice. Add approximately 1½ ounces spiced rum per serving, if desired.

SERVES ABOUT 16

86) FALL TEA PUNCH

4 cups water
2 cups sugar
½ cup fresh lemon juice
4 tea bags (Earl Grey or orange pekoe)
1 teaspoon vanilla extract
1 teaspoon almond extract
2½ liters ginger ale
spiced rum as needed
lemon wedges, for garnish
ground nutmeg, for garnish

Combine the water, sugar, lemon juice, tea bags, and vanilla and
almond extracts in a pot over low heat, and stir until the sugar is
dissolved. Let the tea bags steep for approximately 10 minutes, then
discard. Transfer the liquid to a bowl or other container, cover, and
refrigerate overnight. Add the ginger ale and serve over ice. Add
approximately 1½ ounces spiced rum per serving, if desired. Garnish with lemon wedges and dust with nutmeg.

SERVES ABOUT 18

87) MASALA CHAI

Chai—derived from a South Asian drink—is a black tea mixed with milk, sugar, and a blend of spices.

....

4 cups water
6 black tea bags
1 tablespoon white sugar (or brown, if desired)
4 whole white cardamom pods
4 to 5 whole cloves
1 cinnamon stick, cracked
1½ cups milk
½ cup sweetened condensed milk
spiced liqueur (e.g., Tuaca, Licor 43, or Navan vanilla liqueur),
    if desired
freshly grated nutmeg, for garnish

....

Combine the water, tea bags, sugar, cardamom, cloves, and cinnamon stick in a medium pot and bring to a boil. Remove from heat and let steep for about / minutes. Strain and slowly stir in the milk and condensed milk. Return to the pot and rewarm, if desired. Pour into individual coffee cups. Add ½ to 1 ounce of spiced liqueur to each serving, if desired. Garnish with freshly grated nutmeg.

SERVES ABOUT 6

88) CAPPUCCINO COOLER

3 cups chilled espresso
6 cups milk
2 cups simple syrup (see page 6)
2 cups Starbucks Coffee Liqueur (Godiva Cappuccino Liqueur or
  even Kahlua are also good options) (optional)
espresso beans, for garnish

Combine all of the ingredients except the espresso beans in a large
container and refrigerate until chilled. Pour each serving into a
cocktail shaker with ice and shake to make the mixture a little
frothy. Pour into a highball glass. Garnish each serving with a few
espresso beans.

SERVES ABOUT 12

89) SNOWMAN PUNCH

2 cups water
1 cup sugar
12 whole cloves
1 cinnamon stick
3 pints cranberry juice cocktail
one 12-ounce can frozen lemonade concentrate, thawed
one 12-ounce can frozen orange juice concentrate, thawed
1½ ounces spiced rum per serving (optional)
3 oranges, cut into wheels, for garnish
¼ cup maraschino cherries, for garnish

Combine the water, sugar, cloves, and cinnamon stick in a pot and bring to a boil, stirring until the sugar dissolves. Reduce the heat and simmer for 5 minutes. Cool completely and remove the spices. In a punch bowl, combine the spiced syrup mixture with the cranberry juice cocktail and lemonade and orange juice concentrates with ice. Stir to blend. Serve over ice, adding the spiced rum to individual servings, if desired. Garnish with orange wheels and cherries.

SERVES ABOUT 11

90) Spiced Winter Cider

1 gallon apple cider
5 cinnamon sticks, plus extra for garnish
2 oranges, cut into wheels
1 red apple, cored and sliced
1 green apple, cored and sliced
1½ teaspoons whole cloves
¼ cup dried cranberries
1 to 1½ ounces spiced rum or liqueur (e.g., Tuaca, Captain Morgan, etc.) per serving (optional)

In a large pot, combine the apple cider, cinnamon, fruit, cloves, and dried cranberries and bring to a boil. Reduce the heat and simmer for 8 to 10 minutes. Ladle cider (without spices and fruit) into coffee mugs and serve hot. If desired, add spiced rum or Tuaca to each serving. Garnish with cinnamon sticks.

SERVES ABOUT 16

91) Caramel Apple Cider

Use the same recipe as above, adding 16 caramel candies while heating the mixture. Stir constantly until the caramels are completely dissolved. If desired, add ½ ounce Tuaca or butterscotch schnapps to each serving.

92) SWEDISH GLÖGG

This classic Scandinavian hot drink is traditionally consumed during the holidays. My mother-in-law was gracious enough to give me her "secret" family recipe.

....

2 quarts port wine
2 cups sugar (or 1 cup if using a sweet port wine)
1 cup raisins
1 dozen blanched almonds
1 to 2 cinnamon sticks
1 dozen cracked cardamom pods
1 dozen whole cloves
grated orange zest (from about ¼ orange)
1 pint blended whiskey

....

Combine 1 cup of the port in a pot with the sugar, raisins, almonds, cinnamon, cardamom, cloves, and orange zest over low heat and stir until dissolved, 5 to 7 minutes. Add the remaining port and bring to a boil. Reduce the heat to low, add the whiskey, and continue to warm for a few more minutes. Turn off heat and serve hot. This can also be kept in a Crock-Pot over low heat until ready to serve.

SERVES ABOUT 10

9 3) Festive Wassail

6 cups apple cider
2 cinnamon sticks
2½ cups pineapple juice
2 cups cranberry juice
1½ ounces lemon juice
¼ cup honey
2 teaspoons ground nutmeg
1 teaspoon freshly grated lemon zest
1 orange, cut into wheels
1 lemon, cut into wheels
½ cup whole cranberries
1 ounce brandy or whiskey per serving (optional)

Combine the cider and cinnamon sticks in a saucepan. Bring to a boil, then reduce the heat and simmer for 5 minutes. Add the remaining ingredients except the brandy or whiskey, stir well, and simmer for another 5 minutes. Ladle wassail into mugs, serve hot, and if desired, add the brandy or whiskey to individual servings. If you are planning a party, keep it warm in a Crock-Pot and add the brandy as you ladle individual servings. This will also keep your home smelling like the holidays.

SERVES ABOUT 12

94) HOT TOMATO PUNCH ✳

two 46-ounce cans tomato juice
8 tablespoons (1 stick) butter
1 teaspoon salt
1 teaspoon freshly ground black pepper
1 teaspoon Worcestershire sauce
5 drops Tabasco
1 teaspoon celery seed
½ teaspoon dried oregano

Combine all of the ingredients in a saucepan. Cover and bring to a boil. Reduce the heat and simmer for 12 to 15 minutes. Ladle into coffee mugs and serve hot.

SERVES ABOUT 10

95) Spiced Pear Infusion

This infusion can be used in a variety of rum drinks, both hot and cold, or served with just a simple mixer like ginger ale or juice. It's great to have around the holidays.

4 pears
1 liter 10 Cane rum
3 cinnamon sticks
2 whole anise stars
2 vanilla beans, split lengthwise
1 tablespoon whole cloves
½ cup raisins

To roast the pears, core and halve them and wrap them in aluminum foil. Roast in a preheated 350°F oven for about 25 minutes, or until the pears start to soften and sweat. When cool enough to handle, cut into slices.

In a clean, dry jar, combine the sliced roasted pears and the remaining ingredients. Let sit for at least 48 hours. If a stronger pear flavor is desired, let sit for another 48 hours. Strain and bottle.

96) SPICED PEAR DAIQUIRI

2 ounces Spiced Pear Infusion (see page 120)
1 ounce freshly squeezed lime juice (from about 1 lime)
1 ounce simple syrup (see page 6)
fresh pear slice, for garnish
ground cinnamon, for garnish

Combine the Spiced Pear Infusion, lime juice, and simple syrup in a cocktail shaker with ice. Shake vigorously and strain into a martini glass. Garnish with fresh pear slice and a dust of cinnamon.

SERVES 1

97) SPICED PEAR CIDER

6 to 8 ounces apple cider, heated
1 ounce Spiced Pear Infusion (see page 120)
cinnamon stick, for garnish
pear slice, for garnish

Fill a coffee mug with the hot apple cider and add the Spiced Pear Infusion. Garnish with a cinnamon stick and pear slice.

SERVES 1

98) Mango Vanilla Infusion

This is a great infused rum that can simply be served over ice with 7-Up or fresh sour (see page 6). It was created for 10 Cane rum, a premium rum made from fresh-pressed cane juice.

2 cups diced mango (about 2 medium-sized mangos)
2 vanilla beans, split lengthwise
1 liter 10 Cane rum

In a clean, dry jar, combine the mango and vanilla beans. Add the rum and stir. Close and let sit in a cool, dark area for at least 48 hours. Depending on the ripeness of the mangos, the infusion may need to sit longer for a pronounced mango flavor. Strain and bottle.

99) POLYNESIAN SLING

This is a Mai Tai meets the Singapore Sling.

3 ounces pineapple juice
3 ounces orange juice
1½ ounces Mango Vanilla Infusion (see page 124)
½ ounce orange curaçao
dash of Angostura bitters
skewered orange wedge and maraschino cherry (known as a flag),
  for garnish

In a cocktail shaker, combine the pineapple juice, orange juice, Mango Vanilla Infusion, and orange curaçao with ice. Shake vigorously and strain into a chilled highball glass filled with ice. Top with a dash of Angostura bitters and garnish with the skewered orange-cherry flag.

SERVES 1

100) Pomegranate Mandarin Infusion

This can simply be served over ice with 7-Up or your favorite juice.

4 mandarin oranges
1½ cups pomegranate seeds (about 3 pomegranates)
1 liter premium vodka

To prepare the mandarins, score the skins to release their natural oils. Slice the mandarins into wheels and place them in a clean, dry jar. Add the pomegranate seeds. Pour in the vodka and close. Let infuse in a cool dark area for one week. Strain and bottle.